Instruments of the Orchestra

Jeffery James Reid

NUVISION PUBLISHING

Instruments of the Orchestra

REFERENCES:
THE NEW COLLEGE ENCYCLOPEDIA OF MUSIC
BY J. A. WESTREP AND F. LI. HARRISON

MUSICAL INSTRUMENTS:
A COMPREHENSIVE DICTIONARY
BY SIBYL MARCUSE

Illustrated by nuvisiondesigns.biz
All illustrations are modifications of the original instruments.

Books may be ordered at
amazon.com and barnesandnoble.com

ISBN

PO Box 4455 | Wilmington NC
nuvisiondesigns.biz/publications

Printed in the United States of America.

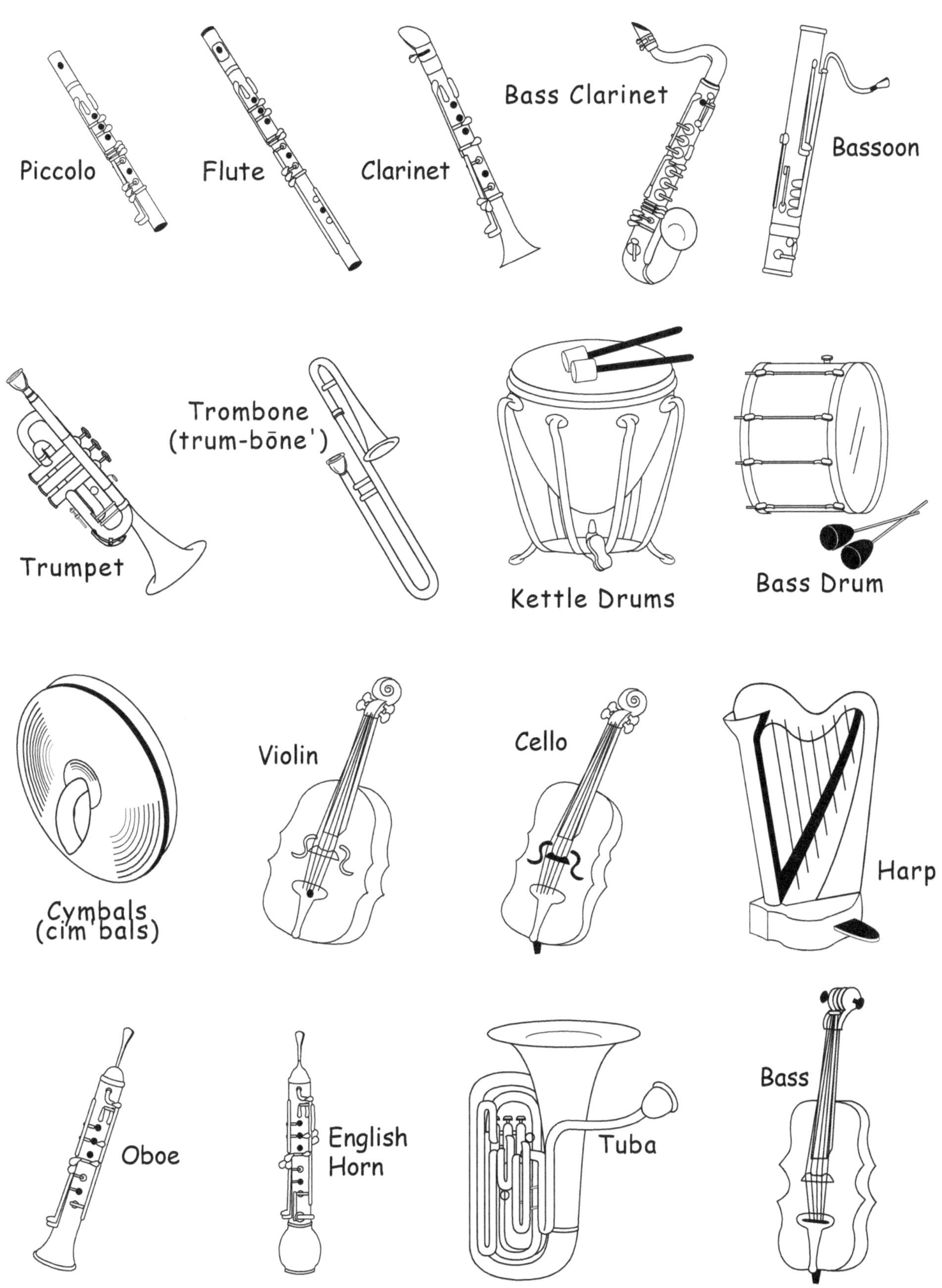

Piccolo
Flute
Clarinet
Bass Clarinet
Bassoon
Trumpet
Trombone
(trum-bōne')
Kettle Drums
Bass Drum
Cymbals
(cim'bals)
Violin
Cello
Harp
Oboe
English
Horn
Tuba
Bass

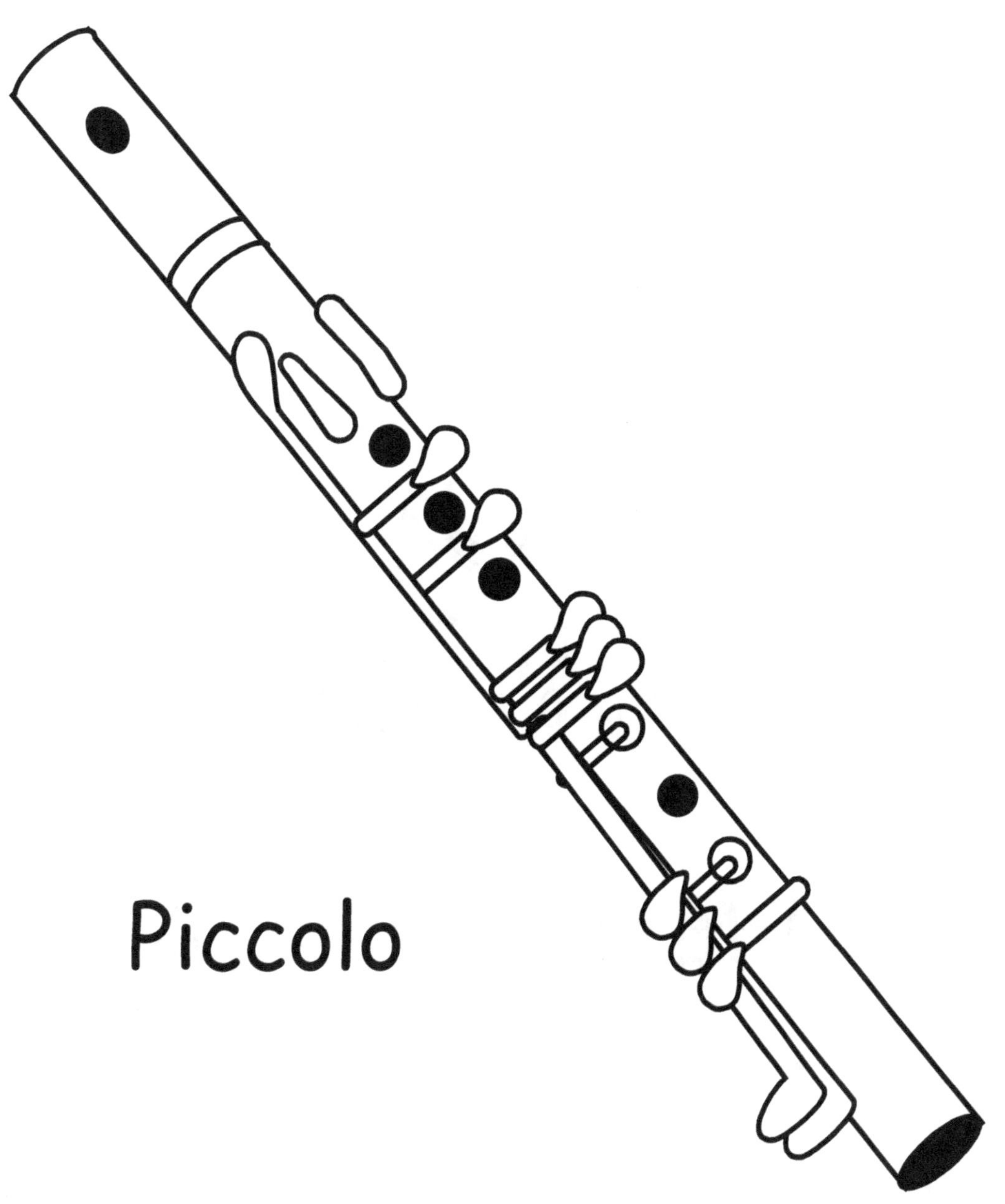

Piccolo

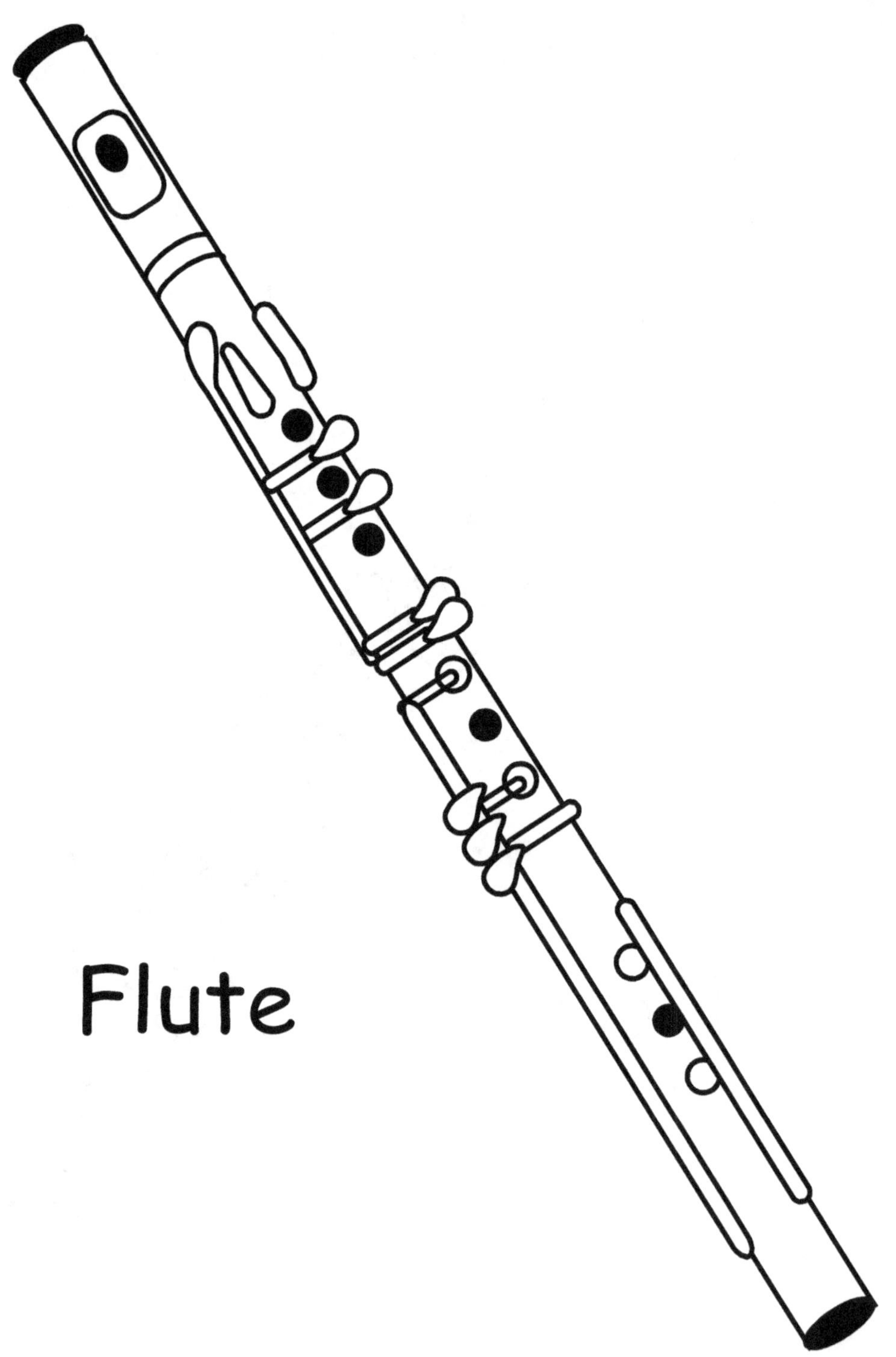

Flute

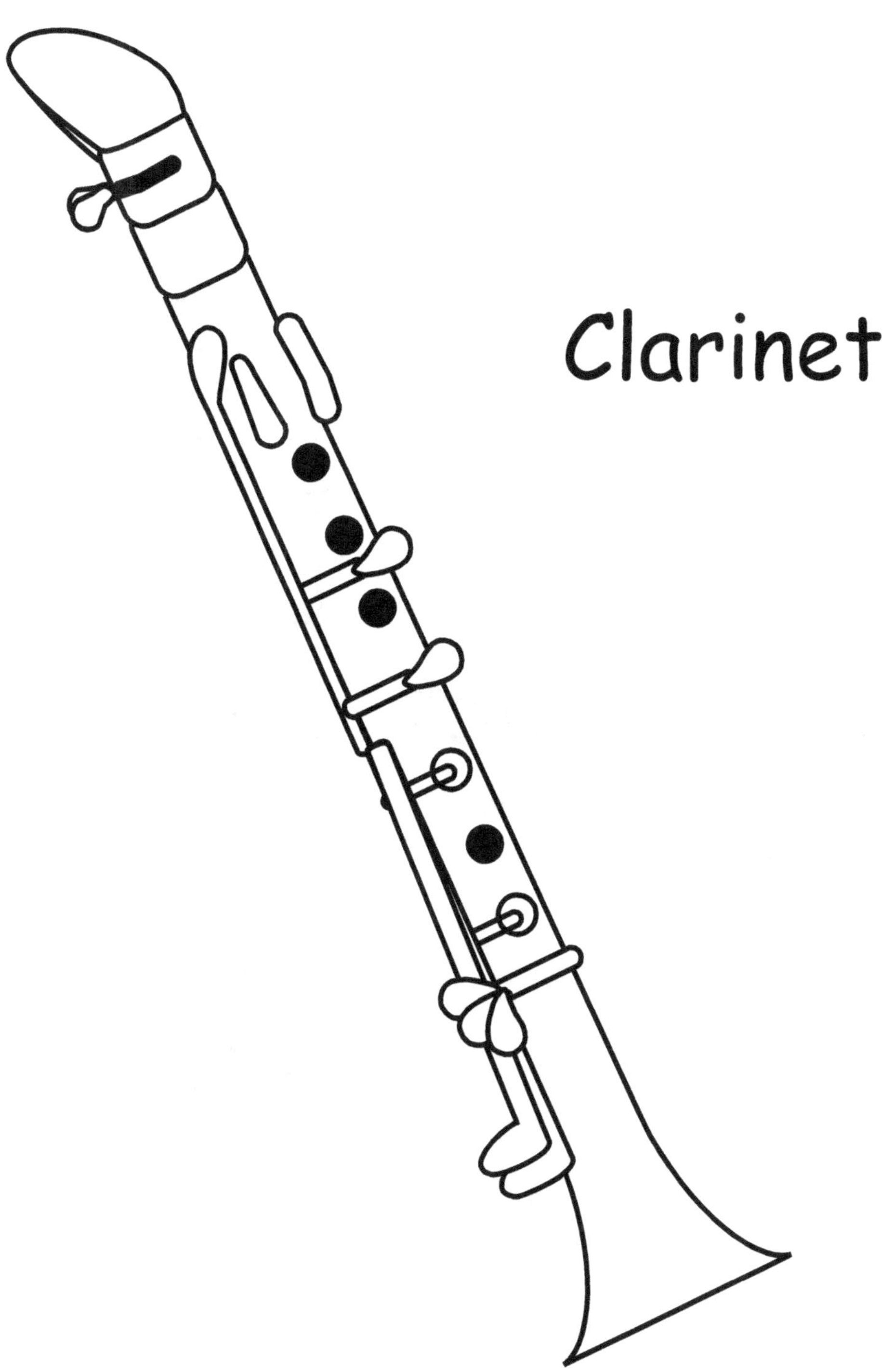

Clarinet

Bass Clarinet

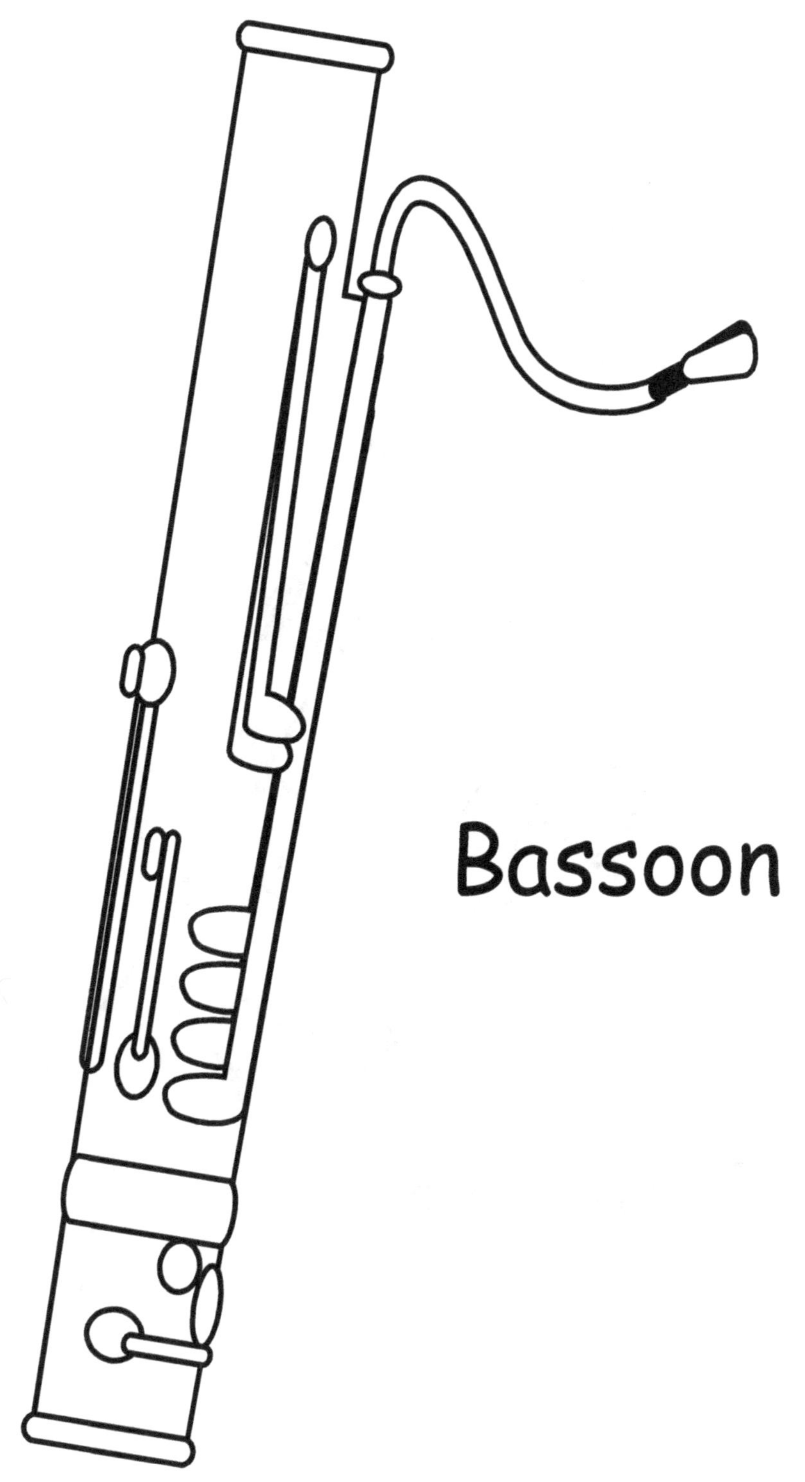

Bassoon

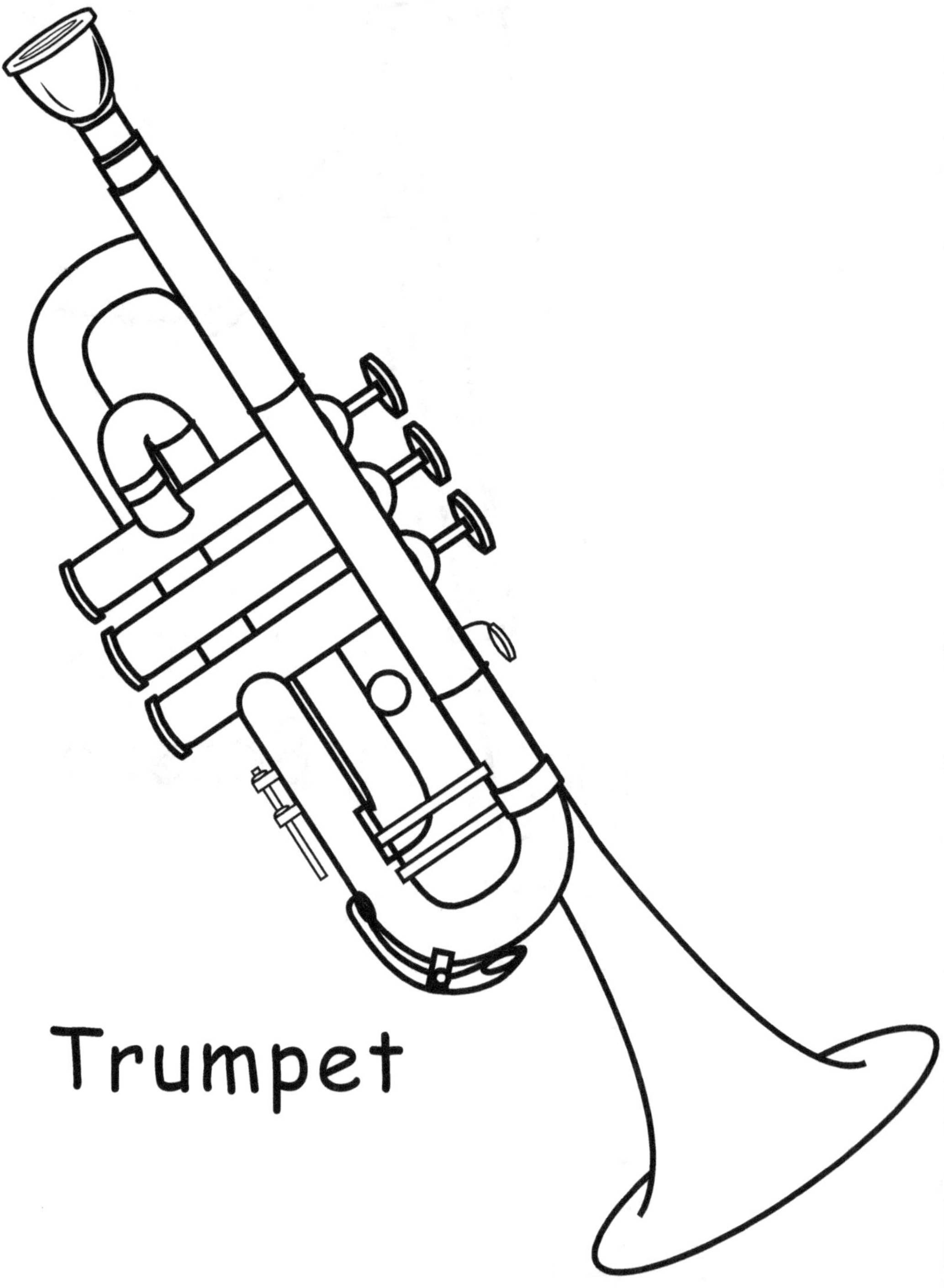

Trumpet

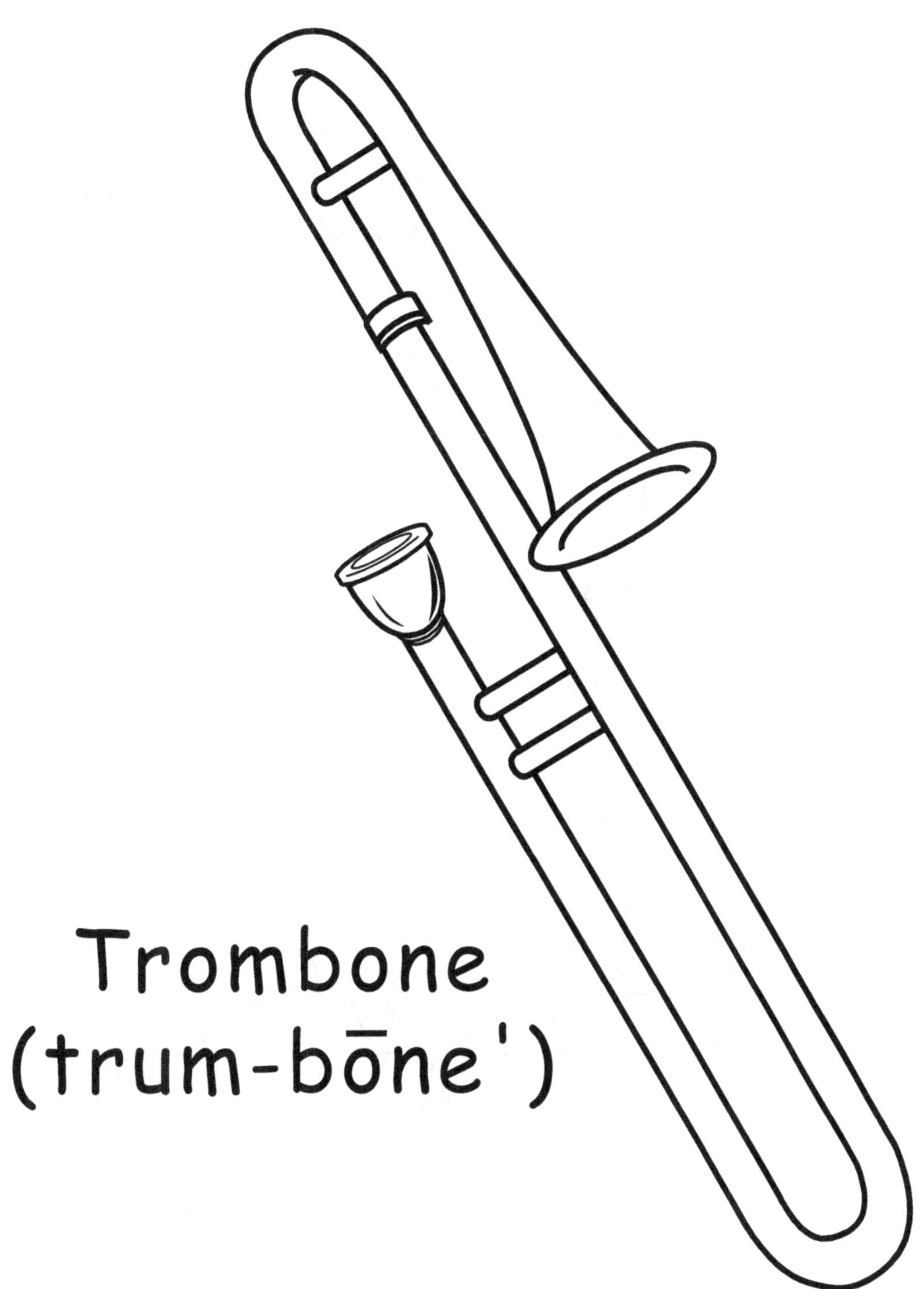

Trombone
(trum-bōne')

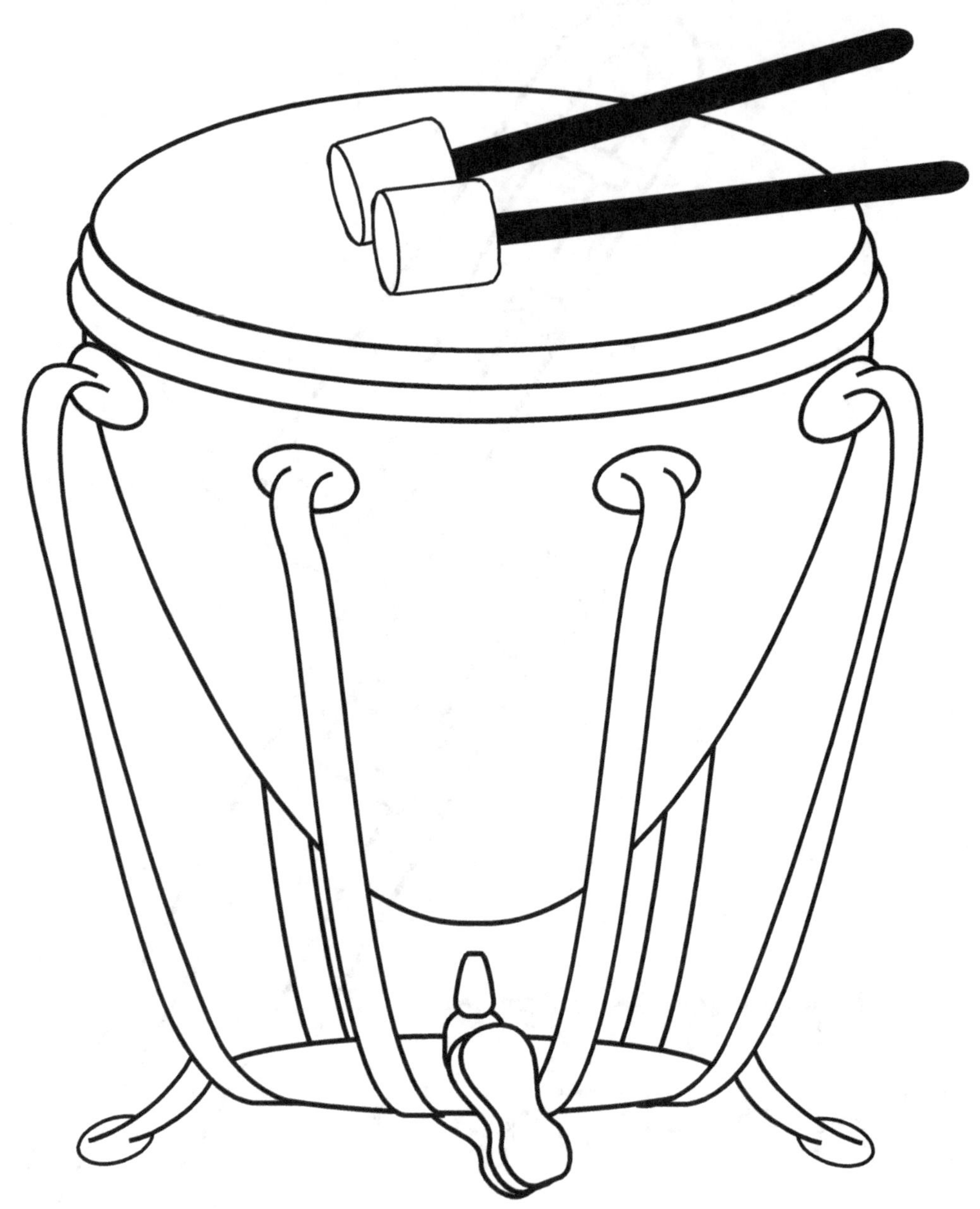

Kettle Drums

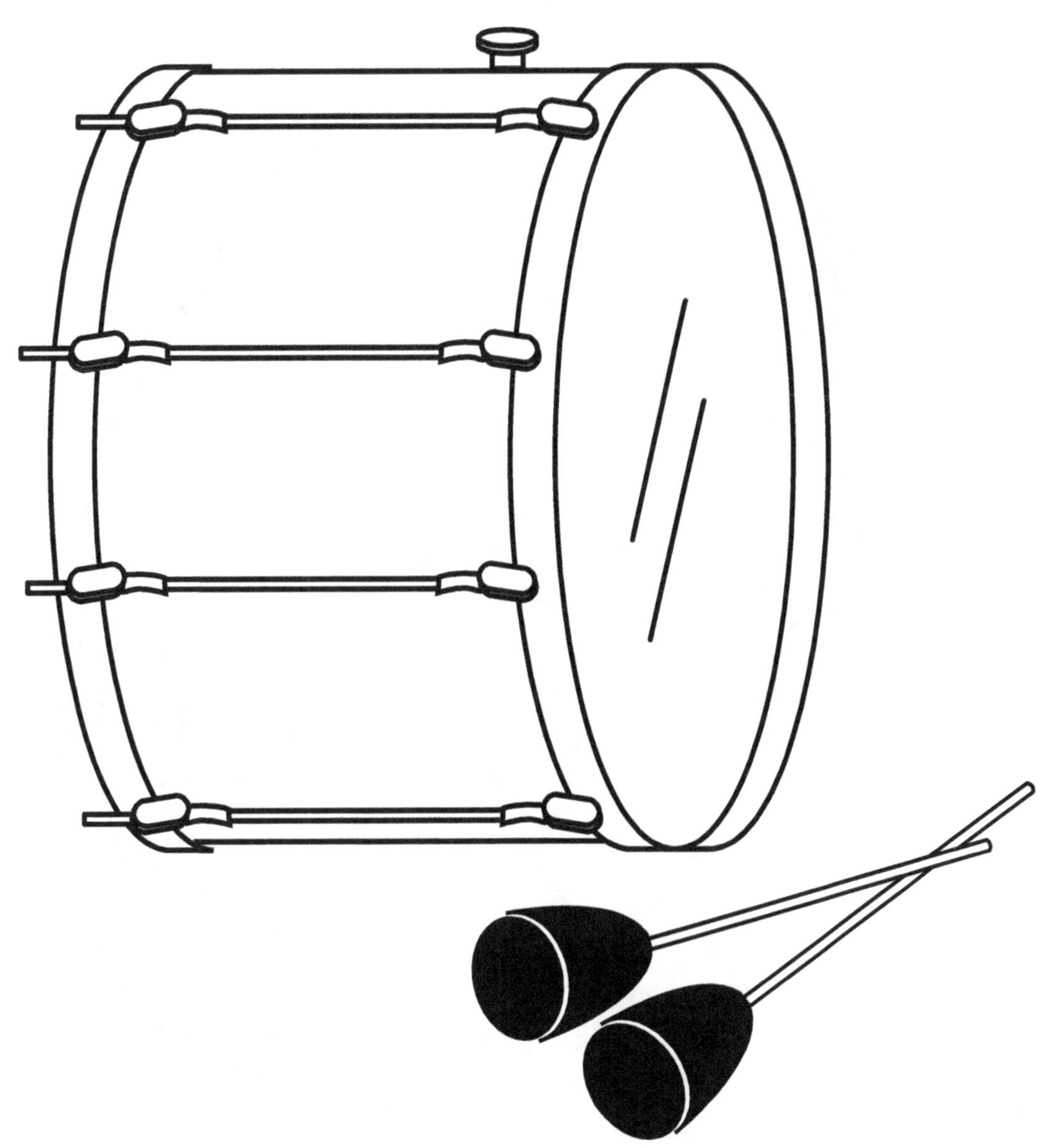

Bass Drum

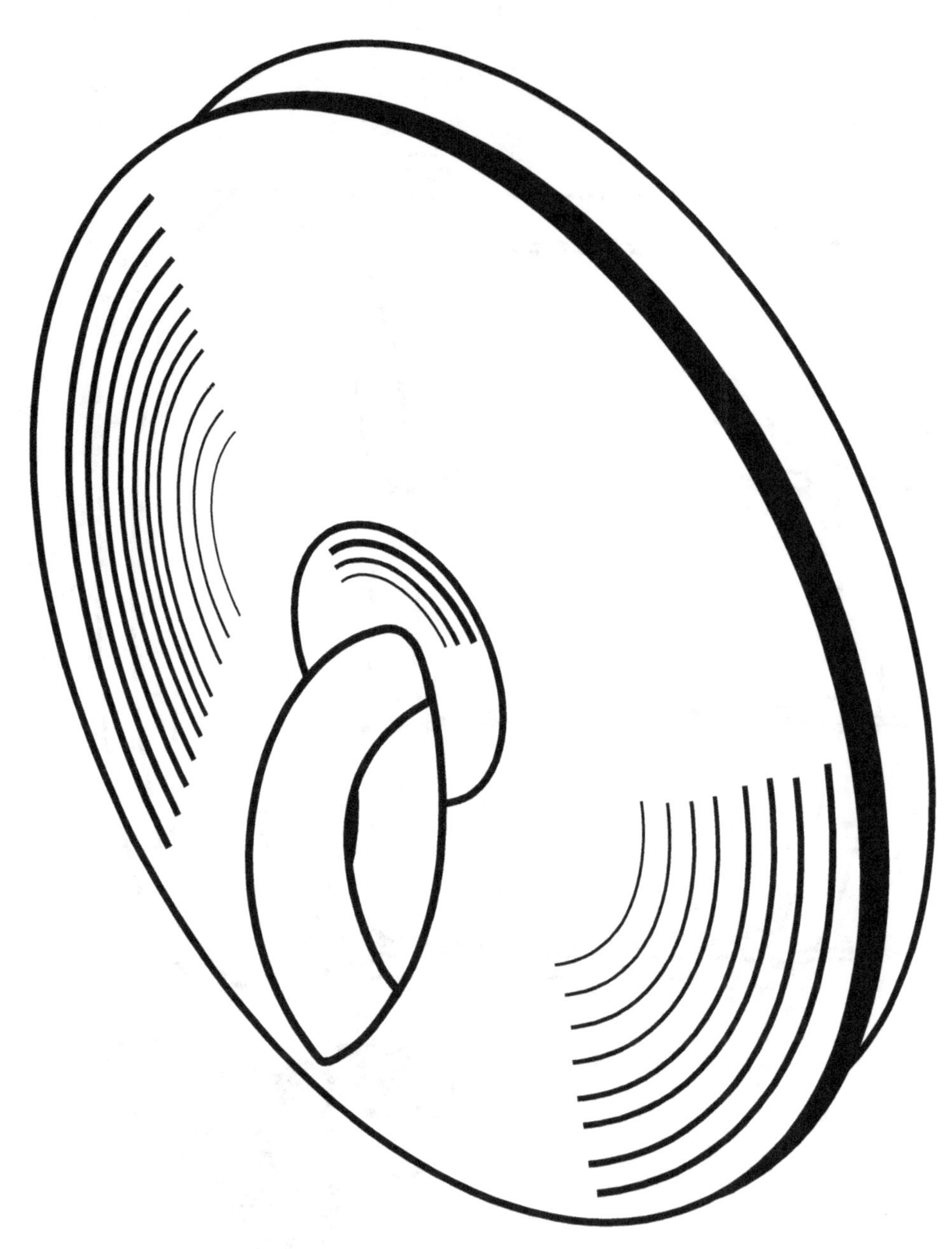

Cymbals
(cim'bals)

Violin

Cello

Harp

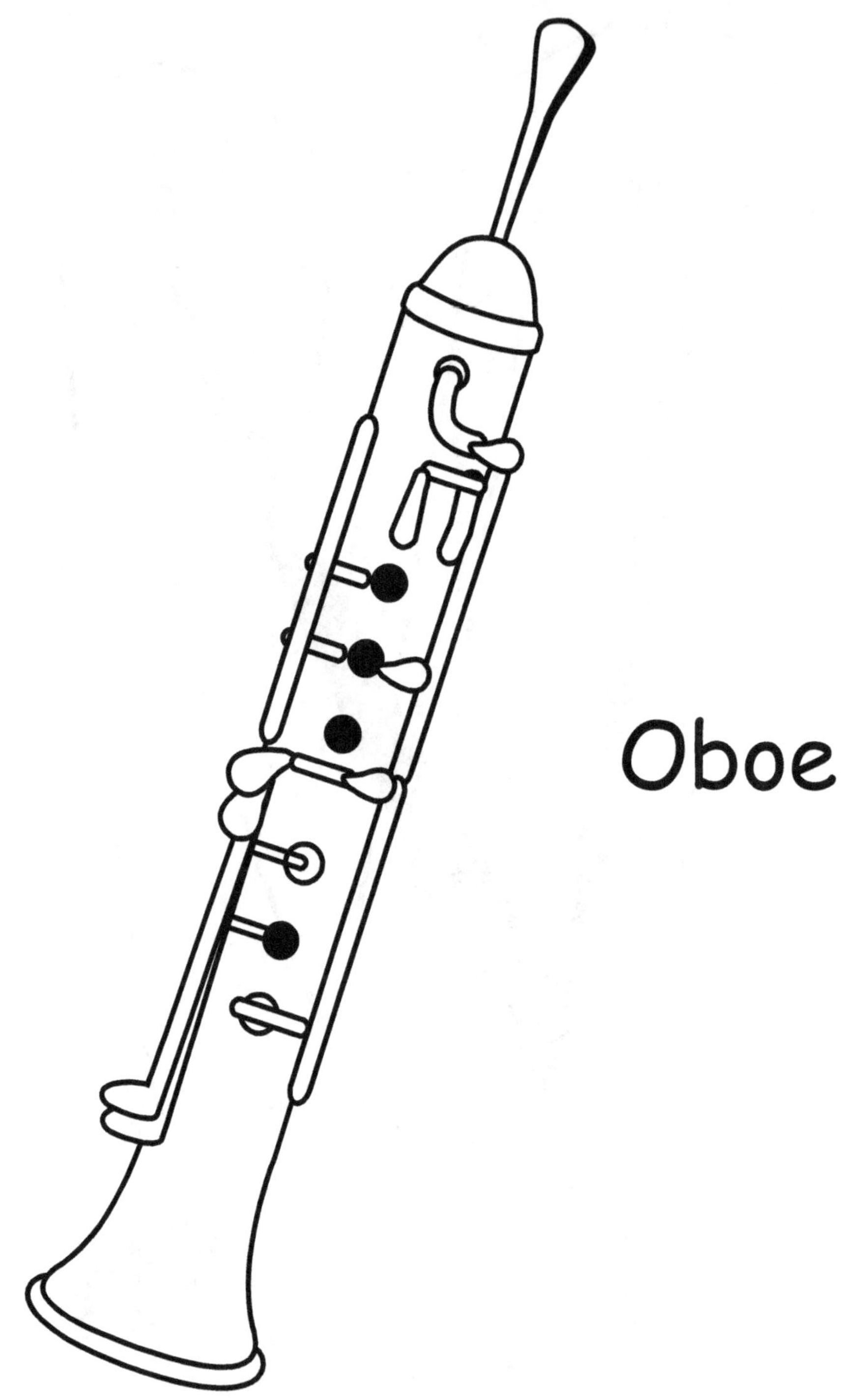

Oboe

English Horn

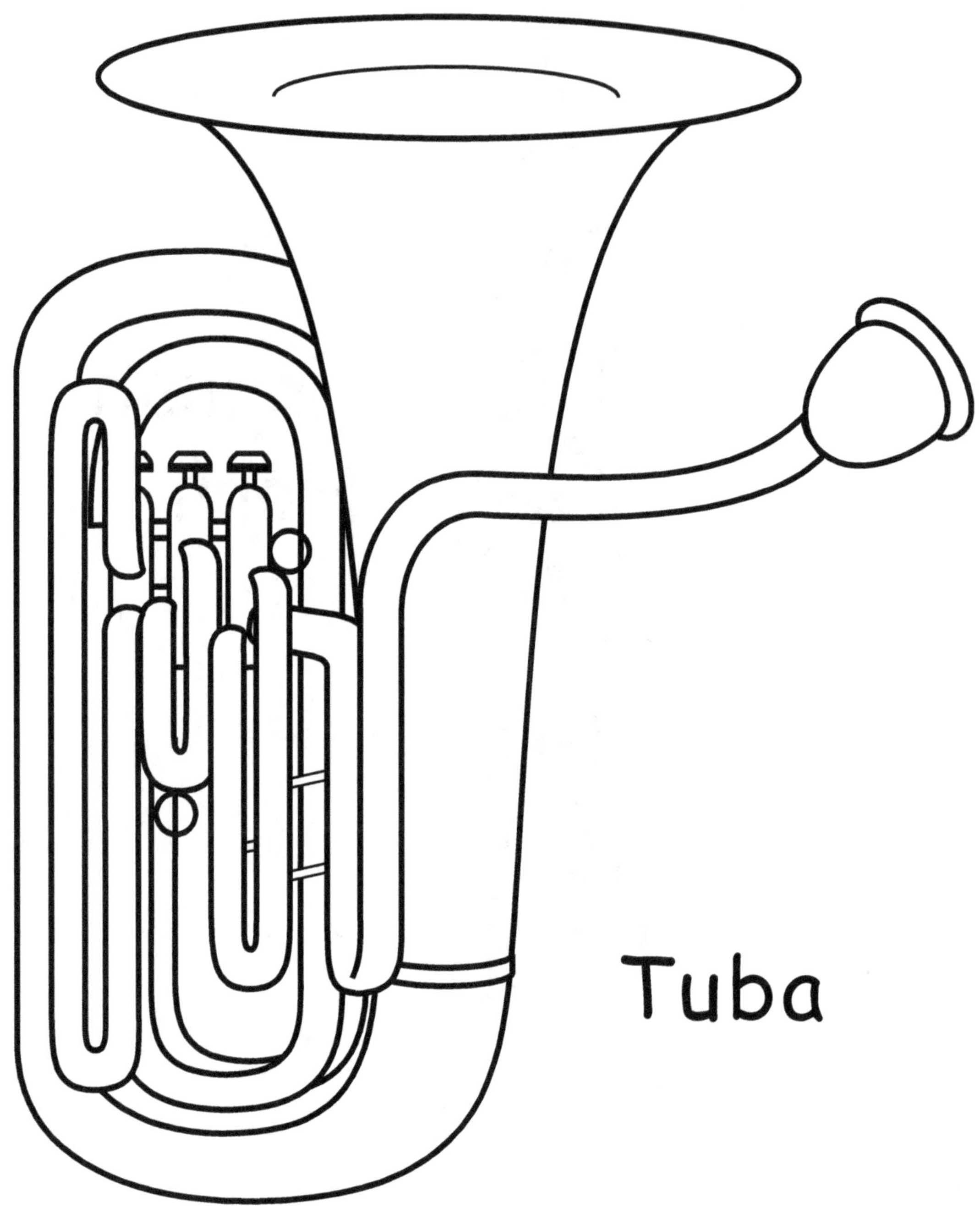

Tuba

Bass

Draw a Harp

Draw an Oboe

Draw Kettle Drums

Instruments of the Orchestra

Name all of the instruments in this coloring book.

1. _______________________   10. _______________________

2. _______________________   11. _______________________

3. _______________________   12. _______________________

4. _______________________   13. _______________________

5. _______________________   14. _______________________

6. _______________________   15. _______________________

7. _______________________   16. _______________________

8. _______________________   17. _______________________

9. _______________________

Instruments of the Orchestra

Crossword puzzle:
Unscramble the words and place them in the crossword puzzle.

ACROSS

1. ttkele umrds_______________
3. booe _______________
5. rpah_______________
9. ssba rumd _______________
10. sabs clarietn _______________
11. lleco_______________
13. lvioin _______________
15. bneoromt_______________

DOWN

2. ymclabs_______________
4. rmuttpe_______________
6. hsilgne rhno _______________
8. neritlac_______________
10. ssabono_______________
12. sabs _______________
14. batu _______________
16. ccloopi_______________
18. tuelf_______________

Instruments of the Orchestra

1. Piccolo
2. Flute
3. Clarinet
4. Bass Clarinet
5. Bassoon
6. Trumpet
7. Trombone
8. Kettle Drums
9. Bass Drum
10. Cymbals
11. Violin
12. Cello
13. Harp
14. Oboe
15. English Horn
16. Tuba
17. Bass

ANSWERS TO SCRAMBLES

ACROSS	DOWN
1. kettle drums	2. cymbals
3. oboe	4. trumpet
5. harp	6. english horn
9. bass drum	8. clarinet
10. bass clarinet	10. bassoon
11. cello	12. bass
13. violin	14. tuba
15. trombone	16. piccolo
	18. flute